BAFFLED BEAR

Written by Keith Faulkner
Illustrated by Manhar Chauham

SIENA

As Brown Bear woke up, the sun was shining through his window. It was a sunny day and, better still, it was a holiday. Brown Bear could do just what he wanted.

He leapt out of bed and opened his cupboard.
"I know what I'll do today. I'll go **fishing**," he said to himself, getting out his fishing things.

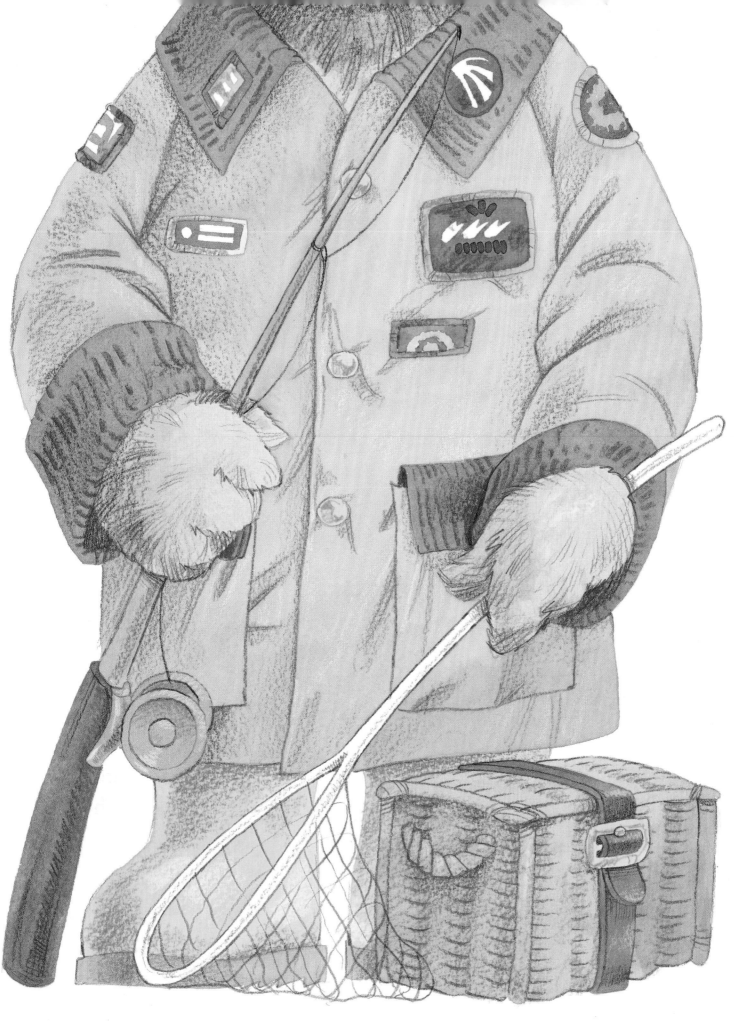

Turn to the back of the book and find Brown Bear's fishing head.

But, by the time Brown Bear had put all his fishing things on, he had changed his mind.

"No, I won't go fishing today," said Brown Bear.
"**Skateboarding**. Yes, that's what I'll do."
So, Brown Bear put away his fishing things and got out his skateboard, pads and helmet.

Turn to the back of the book and find Brown Bear's skateboarding head.

But, just as Brown Bear was ready for skateboading, he
changed his mind again!

"No, I won't go skateboarding today," he thought.

"It's such a lovely day, I'll go **diving** instead."

So, Brown Bear put away all his skateboarding things and
got out his snorkel, mask and flippers, ready to go diving.

Turn to the back of the book and find Brown Bear's diving head.

But, no sooner had Brown Bear dressed in all his diving things, he changed his mind once again.
"No, I really don't feel like diving today," he said. "I feel more like walking."

"I know, I'll go **hiking**," he suddenly decided.
So, Brown Bear got out all his hiking things.

Turn to the back of the book and find Brown Bear's hiking head.

Dressed in all his hiking things, with his backpack on,
Brown Bear opened his front door.
"Oh dear!" he said. "It's beginning to get dark. It's too late
to go hiking today."

So, Brown Bear put on his dressing gown, made a mug
of hot chocolate, and settled down in his comfy chair to
read a good book.
"I know what I'll do today," he chuckled to himself.
"I think I'll just do some **relaxing**." he said with a smile.

Turn to the back of the book and find Brown Bear's relaxing head.

Choose the heads to complete the pictures of Bear in the story.

Fishing

Skateboarding

Diving

Hiking

Relaxing